Charles George Gordon

Reflections in Palestine

1883

Charles George Gordon

Reflections in Palestine
1883

ISBN/EAN: 9783337281182

Printed in Europe, USA, Canada, Australia, Japan

Cover: Foto ©ninafisch / pixelio.de

More available books at **www.hansebooks.com**

REFLECTIONS IN PALESTINE.

1883.

BY

CHARLES GEORGE GORDON.

London:
MACMILLAN AND CO.
1884.

The Right of Translation and Reproduction is Reserved.

PREFATORY NOTE.

THE following pages are given to the public not only with the sanction of General Gordon, but by his express wish and injunction. Their contents are the fruits of meditation and inquiry during his prolonged sojourn in the Holy Land from January to December, 1883. The notes are not cast into a perfectly connected form. They have been revised with anxious care by more than one of the writer's friends, and he is not responsible for the precise shape and order in which they have been collected and arranged.

General Gordon's belief is that they

will be of use in awakening new thoughts in religious minds, and stirring a spirit of faithful investigation. In this belief he had the publication of the present volume much at heart down to the very eve of his departure for Kartoum. His interest in the matter has not abated since. In the midst of the heavy responsibilities of his post on the Nile, he still turns to the topics that filled his mind last year.

So late as the 3rd of March, 1884, only five weeks ago, he wrote as follows from Kartoum :—

"The title is correct; I am very in-
"terested in the book, for it may tend to
"show forth God's dwelling in us. This
"is the great secret (Psalm xxv.). Also
"He made us in order to have a house
"—naos—to live in. Without us He is
"houseless; He needs us, and how much
"do we need Him! I am comforted here
"in my weakness by the reflection that
"our Lord rules all things; and it is dire
"rebellion to dislike or murmur against

" His rule. May His Name be glorified!
" these people blessed and comforted!
" and may I be deeply humbled, and thus
" have a greater sense of His indwelling
" Spirit! This is my earnest prayer."

A wish so strongly and deliberately expressed by such a man as General Gordon deserves to be respected, and it is in compliance with it that these notes are now published.

April 9, 1884.

ADDENDUM.

On the 6th of March General Gordon wrote to a friend from Kartoum :—

" I refer to Colonel Sir Charles Warren, R.E., Brompton Barracks, Chatham, for the explanation of the plan of Jerusalem without *débris*, which is in his book, 'The Temple and the Tomb.' His plan shows very clearly the human figure, and only wants the skull hill to be considered with it to complete it.

"Two passages—2 Chronicles xiv. 11, and 2 Chronicles xx. 12—are helpful to me this day under my present difficulties.

"Yours sincerely,

"C. G. GORDON."

TABLE OF CONTENTS.

TOPOGRAPHICAL.

	PAGES
THE PLACE OF CRUCIFIXION	1—3
THE HARAM AND GREAT ALTAR	4
OUTLINE OF THE TEMPLE	5
CHIEF ARTICLES OF SERVICE	6
THE ROCK AND THE CUP	7
THE EASTERN AND WESTERN HILLS	8—10
BOUNDARY OF JUDAH ON THE NORTH	11—17
ENSHEMESH	18

RELIGIOUS.

PREFATORY PRAYER	19
THE WRITTEN WORD	19—23
FIRST THREE DAYS OF CREATION	23—28
BAPTISM	29—39
THE PRESENCE OF THE HOLY GHOST	40—46
HOLY COMMUNION	47—60
"TAKE, EAT"	65—68
THE TONGUE	68—74

b

TABLE OF CONTENTS.

	PAGES
FRUIT	74—76
"DYING THOU SHALT DIE"	76—78
SALVATION	81—86
THE NEW BIRTH	87—96
WARNING TO THE WATCHMEN	97—100
INDWELLING IN US AS LIVING VESSELS	100—104
COMFORT THROUGH OUR PARDON IN CHRIST	105—109
THE PASSION OF CHRIST	109—118
PRAYER	119, 120
CHARACTERS IN HOLY SCRIPTURE	121—124

REFLECTIONS IN PALESTINE.

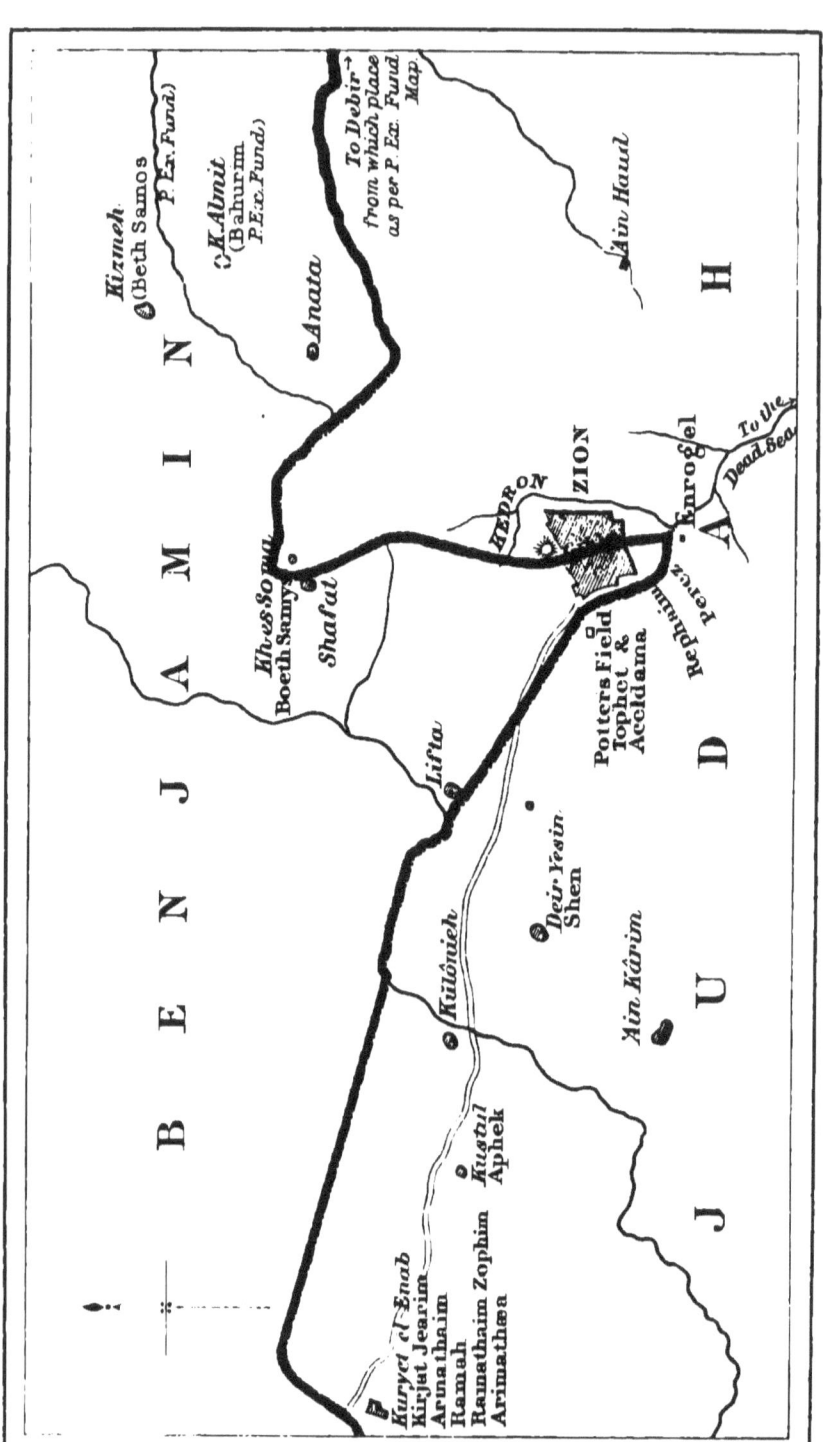

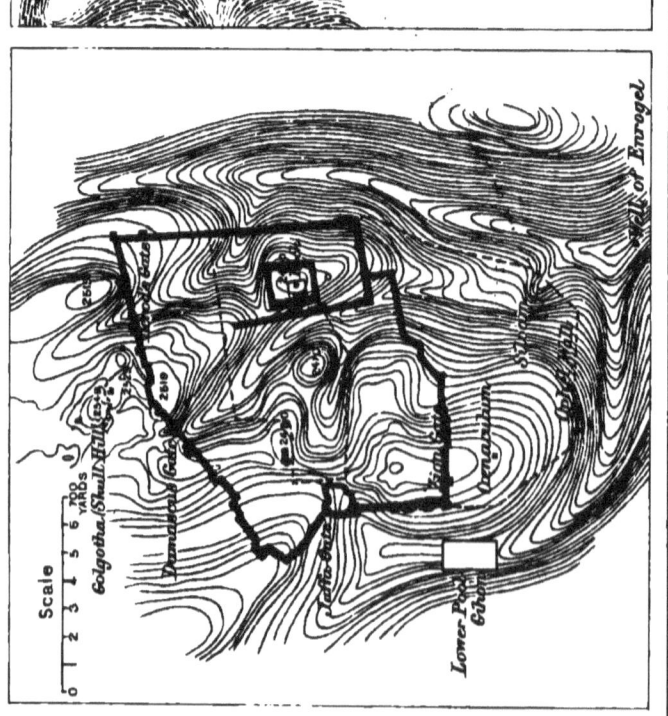

REFLECTIONS SUGGESTED IN PALESTINE.

TOPOGRAPHICAL.

THE PLACE OF CRUCIFIXION.

THE eastern and more sacred of the two hills on which Jerusalem is built rises to an average height throughout its whole range, which is rather lower than that of the average height, taken similarly, of the west hill. We trace its course as a ridge running north and south, with steep flanks, and ending in a somewhat sharp declivity toward the south. The north end expands until it forms part of the almost level plateau north of the city.

This northern end is, however, marked by an apex of uncovered rock—a rocky knoll resembling in form the human skull

—and from this "skull hill" the crown or ridge of this eastern hill follows a line which is aslant, or askew, to the valley of the Kedron until it reaches, at about two-thirds of its entire length, another bare rock, now covered by the Mosque of Omar. The crucifixion seems to have been on the skull hill, and the great altar of burnt sacrifice to have been on this second remarkable rock within the temple enclosure. Beyond, or to the north of the skull hill, the present slaughter-house of the city is placed, and a continuous tradition connects that portion of ground outside the northern wall with the place of stoning. Adjoining this hill, but not under it, is the large cavern containing a vast cistern which is known as the grotto of Jeremiah.

I think that the cross stood on the top of the skull hill, in the centre of it, and not where the slaughter-house now stands. Leviticus i. 11 says that the victim was to be slain "on the side of the altar, northward before the Lord," and literally they were to slay the victims "slantwise to the altar northwards." The altar was on the second knoll within the Haram enclosure, and if the cross were placed in the centre of the skull hill, the whole city, and even the Mount of Olives, would be embraced by those stretched out arms. "All the day long I have stretched forth my hands unto a disobedient and gainsaying people" (Romans x. 21, from Isaiah lxv. 2). Here, also, after that time, at the skull hill, close to the slaughter-house of Jerusalem, were the head-quarters of Titus. I think that Titus put his tent under the brow of the hill, so as to be under cover. Long before, in the cave, Jeremiah had written his Lamentations. *There* Christ suffered without the gate.

When we look from thence at the two hills—the east hill and the west hill—we see that now the west hill is busier than ever. The east hill is almost a field. Corn is grown within the walls of the city, in patches all along and amidst the portion of the modern city north of the Haram.

At the Haram itself there is ample space for the Temple to have been built, with its porch, its holy place, its holy of holies, at some distance from the altar of burnt sacrifice. The outline of Herod's Temple, as seen from the Mount of Olives, must have been very remarkable: an outline quite distinct from that usually assigned to it. We have the great altar—

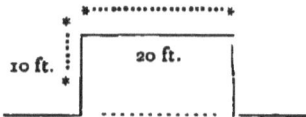

and, after a space, the lofty porch, then much lower, the holy place, and beyond this the veil and holy of holies—

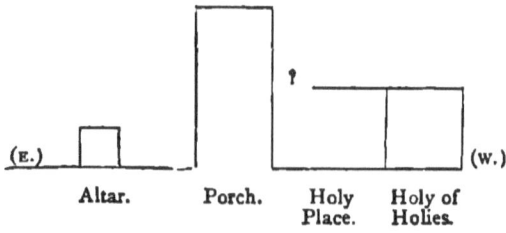

The cube of the holy of holies is well known, but there is a difference which is noticeable between the altar in the Tabernacle and the altar in the Temple. In the Tabernacle the proportion is 5 × 5 × 3. In the Temple 20 × 20 × 10. Since all is quadrupled, why not 20 × 20 × 12? The answer is that the missing 2 cubits were made up by the rock itself. The cubit is 16 inches. The level of the court of the Sakrah is 2,440 feet above the Mediterranean, and the holy of holies was on a lower level, due west of the porch.

There existed also, both in the Tabernacle and in the Temple, an exact measure of distance, and a relative proportion between the chief articles of service, which is instructive.

The Ark of the Covenant was in a direct line with the altars of incense and of burnt offering, while a transverse line at right angles to the first line passed from the golden candlestick through the altar of incense to the table of shewbread.

Thus—

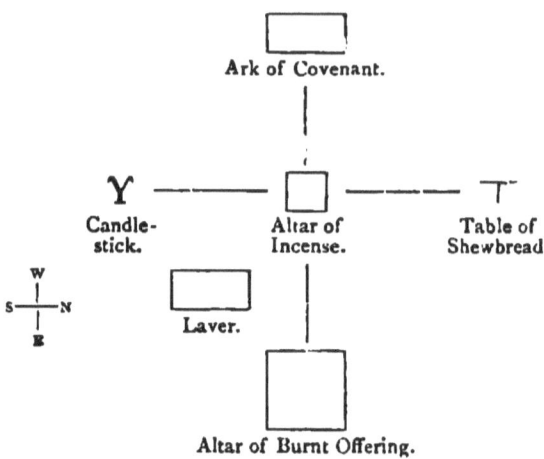

The laver or brazen sea was ten cubits in diameter, and placed "on right side of house eastwards over against the south" (1 Kings vii. 39), or "on the right side of the east end over against the south" (2 Chron. iv. 10). The Caliph, who erected the fountain El Kas, appears to have intended it to occupy the same place as the laver, and to hold about the same quantity. El Kas means the chalice; and I next call your attention to the present wailing-place of the Jews which is opposite this cup or fountain. It is certain that the brazen sea or laver was the first utensil used in the Jewish Church, and it is in our Christian Church the font that is the first utensil used. Also of all the utensils in the Jewish Church left to the Christian Church, we have only the font and the table of the Lord. In Christ's body mystical we have indeed the veil rent asunder in His torn flesh, and in our Church we have the ten commandments beside the Lord's table, but the font and the table of the Lord are the two visible and constant articles of service in our Christian Churches.

I repeat that to my mind the rock and the cup are the only two remnants of the old Temple in the Haram, and they represent the altar-table of the Lord, and the brazen sea or font. The root principle for the right study of Jerusalem is that we should first know our Bibles, and with this knowledge examine the localities. The whole outline of this sacred eastern hill, lying opposite the Mount of Olives, bears a rough resemblance to the human form. From the skull hill, on the north-north-west, the body lies—as did that of the victim—aslant or askew to the altar of burnt sacrifice. This resemblance has become clearer through the investigation of the central (Tyropœon) valley. I cannot, however, do more than leave this subject in its rough outline. It is, throughout, a portion of those thoughts which arise from and turn again towards the place of crucifixion.

The Eastern and Western Hills.

For the sake of clearness I will speak of the two hills covered by the modern city of Jerusalem as the eastern and western hills. The eastern hill fronts the Mount of Olives along its whole eastern flank, bounding the valley of the Kedron. The western is divided from it by a valley, which, in the contour plan of isometric lines of ten feet, is shown to be a deep valley, and this western hill is again bounded to the west and south by another valley, so that the eastern and western hills must at all periods within the limits of history have been sharply distinguishable as tongues or promontories trending southwards from an elevated and comparatively plain plateau north of the city.

In the Bible there is a marked distinction between these two hills, and the eastern has been regarded throughout as the more sacred. Along its eastern flank there are two marked points. Of these the more northerly is that where, near the northern boundary of the Haram, there are signs (as noted in the annexed plan of "Jerusalem without *débris*") of a natural ravine or depression in this flank or side of the hill: the other point is of a different character. It is that indicated in Nehemiah iii. 28, 2 Chronicles xxiii. 15, as "*the horse gate.*" From this point the northern portion of the valley of the Kedron was considered " clean," or "holy," and the southern portion from that point "unholy," or polluted. On this note Jeremiah (xxxi. 40) says that "the whole valley of the dead bodies, and "of the ashes, and all the fields unto the "brook Kedron, unto the corner of the "horse gate towards the east, shall be holy "to the Lord:" as if the valley south of the horse gate, that is south of the temple area, had before been polluted, and this would account for the polluted things which were cast into the brook Kedron by Josiah (2 Kings xxiii. 4). I imagine north of the horse gate the Kedron was holy, south of it it was unholy. I state this because it is generally taken that all Kedron was polluted, but Jeremiah would imply that it was only up to the horse gate. One cannot imagine that the ground east of the temple itself would be "unholy." I have a belief that near the horse gate was the debouch of the offal conduit from "the altar." Under Solomon's stables is a conduit which I expect comes from the well of spirits under the rock. If the rock was "the altar," then into the "well of spirits" went the blood, which is the life — the animal life — and so out into the Kedron valley.

The Kedron commences in a north-east direction near the so-called tomb of the kings. The Kedron, as a boundary, would cut Judah out of the possession of Jerusalem entirely, and I discover no sign of the Kedron having been used as a tribal boundary.

This I regard as important.

It seems that in the divisions recorded in Joshua xv.—xix., the whole land was partitioned and allotted, irrespective of the Jebusites, or other older tribes who may have retained for a time portions of "the promised land." Hence, also, I gather that, while in Scripture we find no mention, by name, of the Tyropœon Valley, or valley between the eastern and the western hills,

we yet are expressly told (Joshua xv. 7)
"the border passed toward the waters of
En-shemesh, and the goings out thereof
were at En-rogel." As to En-rogel there
seems to be no doubt. If we read attentively the record in Joshua xviii. 16, of the
tribal border of Benjamin, we see the
reason for this certainty as to En-rogel.
"The" Benjamite "border came down to
"the end of the mountain that lieth before
"the valley of the son of Hinnom, and
"which is in the valley of the giants on the
"north, and descended to the valley of
"Hinnom, to the side of Jebusi on the south,
"and descended to En-rogel." En-rogel,
or "the fuller's fountain," is thus fixed as
a known site, and I think that in the earlier
passage in Joshua (xv. 7) the expression
"the goings out" means a descent. I said
that the Kedron valley, on the north-east
of the city, commences in a north-east
direction near the so-called tombs of
the kings. Still north of this I observe that there is a large cistern on

the top of Khurbet es Soma. I also observe an exceedingly deep cistern under the so-called "grotto of Jeremiah." I do not, however, know whether there is an ingress from its northern side, or an exit from its southern side. Generally, also, the features of the ground north of Jerusalem prove that the valley of the Kedron would not take the drainage of the northern area, but that for a considerable distance—half a mile or more from the northern (Damascus) gate of the modern city—water would flow down the valley between the eastern and western hills. This watercourse has been artificially diverted, but the valley itself is very deep. Its depth below the summit of the eastern hill near the Haram is very considerable. Hence the rushings forth (rushed out, יֵצְאוּ were from the north It is observable that in Joshua xv. 7, the name "waters of Ain Shemesh" precedes the name "Ain Rogel," and presumably Ain Shemesh is to be found at some other place than that usually assigned to it. I would place it at Khurbet es Soma, and the fountain of the waters of Nephtoah, mentioned in Joshua xv. 9, at Ain Lifta, two miles and a half north-westward of Jerusalem, and there is much else which shows that the line between the tribes of Judah and Benjamin was drawn along the centre of this deep valley between the eastern and western hills of Jerusalem.

The words of Psalm lxxviii. 68, are literally true, "God chose the tribe of Judah, the Mount Zion which He loved." The Hebrew "tsion" is always the eastern hill, and this hill is within the territory of the tribe of Judah. The Septuagint of 2 Chronicles xxxii. 4, says, that "Hezekiah collected many people, and stopped the wells of water, and the river that flowed, or made a division through the city." This is clear enough. It could not be the Kedron, for the lexicon gives to the word used ("diorisonta") the force of "dividing by limits," and this in

Hezekiah's time agrees with all else that the Scripture says of the growth of Jerusalem during his reign.

I believe Hezekiah brought water to the huge cistern under the grotto of Jeremiah, and under Skull Hill, or Golgotha, and thence down "the conduit" to "the inspector's gate" of the temple area.

It would be quite easy to bring the water down, but I could not see the traces of the conduit. Near Skull Hill, to the west, is the place which Conder describes in the "Quarterly Statement of the Palestine Exploration Fund" for last April [1883]. I went there to-day and saw some fine carved bits of stone, vine leaves, and pomegranates, and a segment of a circular building, with a thirty-six feet radius. There is one tomb, and it is 200 yards west of Jeremiah's grotto.

The western hill of Jerusalem was probably at first inhabited by the Gibeonites. I do not believe in the Gibeahs, Gibeons, and Mizpahs of the Concordances. There is a strange mixture in these terms, and one cannot well distinguish the exact locality, but other passages show where the Gibeonites dwelt. Their character was treacherous, and this remained a distinguishing feature of those who lived on the west hill.

Joshua (ix. 23) sentences them "to be hewers of wood and drawers of water to the congregation," and (verse 27) "for the altar of the Lord in the place the Lord should choose,"—a peculiar sentence if the Gibeonites lived far from the intended site of the temple, but not so if they lived near it, on the western hill.

Joshua's journey from Gilgal to defend the Gibeonites shows this. The line of his attack upon Adonizedek, king of Jebus, specifies his night march, his route, and his attack at dawn close to Gibeon.

In the book of Judges i. 4—7, it is remarkable that Judah takes Bezek, and after this it is said that he brought Adoni-bezek to Jerusalem; so it would seem that Bezek was Jerusalem—that is, the east hill, which Judah took, killed its king, and left desolate. I could refer also to Judges xix. xx., but I pass on.

Next come Jonathan's provocation of the Philistines and the renewal of the kingdom at Gilgal. After it (1 Samuel xiii. 15) Samuel arose and went up from Gilgal to Gibeah of Benjamin. At Gibeah Saul numbered the people—about 600 men—and the expulsion of the Philistines from the western hills was the first step towards the re-conquest of Jebus, which David completed. The general impression from these and other passages is that the Gibeah of Benjamin and the Gibeah of Saul are the same place, and that this is this west hill of Jerusalem, the place whence Saul went out, and to which he returned (1 Sam. xxii. 6).

I hope I have made it clear that the right apprehension of the boundaries for Judah and Benjamin, as given in Joshua

xv. and xviii., turns on whether we put En-shemesh at Ain Haud to the east of the temple, or at Khurbet es Soma (Beth Samys), to the north of the temple. This is the point. If the question of boundary is settled the others fall in in sequence.

RELIGIOUS.

ALMIGHTY FATHER, who knowest the secrets of all hearts, vouchsafe to reveal Thyself unto us in these pages, so far as they are in accordance with Thy Word, for the sake of our Lord and Saviour Jesus Christ, who liveth and reigneth with Thee, and the Holy Ghost, One God, world without end. *Amen.*

THE WRITTEN WORD IS THE SHEATH OR VEHICLE OF THE INCORRUPTIBLE WORD.

"All Scripture is given by inspiration of God, and is profitable . . . for instruction in righteousness."—2 Tim. iii. 16. Bibles abound in our land, but are they read and studied as they ought to be, considering who is the writer? It is said, both in the Old and the New Testament, "Man shall not live by bread alone, but by every word that proceedeth out of the mouth of God."—Matt. iv. 4, and Deut. viii. 3. How few forget to take their daily meals? yet we starve our souls, though they require their portion which is the Word of God. We know no more how it nourishes our spiritual nature than we do how our bodies are benefited by the food we take in. "So is the kingdom of God, as if a man should cast seed into the ground; and should sleep, and rise night and day, and the seed should spring and grow up, he knoweth not how."—Mark iv. 26, 27. "The seed is the word of God."—Luke viii. 11. May not the reason that there are such differences of opinion on religion be, that commentaries and other writings of *man* are read and studied instead of the Scriptures searched? "The things of God knoweth no man, but the Spirit of God"—1 Cor. ii. 11; and He alone can reveal His own words: "YE DO ERR, NOT KNOWING THE SCRIPTURES"—Matt. xxii. 29.

In family and public worship how little is read of the Bible, compared with man's words. Take a sermon which lasts from twenty minutes to an hour; as a rule, a single verse or two is taken, and the preacher's opinion on that text occupies the time; verses may be brought in here and there to support his argument. Isolated passages of the Bible, and detached portions, may be made to support almost any opinion. The outward letter of the Scriptures is but the sheath or vehicle of the incorruptible Word, by which, as Peter testifies, we are born again of God.—1 Peter i. 23. Surely, that portion of the Bible which teaches us that Hagar's and Sarah's history was an allegory, is intended by the Holy Ghost as a key to understand all the

Scriptures. He will keep us from becoming fanciful in our interpretation, if we look prayerfully to Him for His teaching. "Who teacheth like Him."— Job xxxvi. 22. Paul says: "We speak, not in the words which man's wisdom teacheth, but which the Holy Ghost teacheth; comparing spiritual things with spiritual."— 1 Cor. ii. 13. "I will make known my words unto you." — Prov. i. 23. "I will show thee that which is noted in the scripture of truth."—Dan. x. 21. "The holy scriptures are able to make thee wise unto salvation."—2 Tim. iii. 15. "Then opened he their understanding, that they might understand the scriptures."—Luke xxiv. 45. This opening of the Scriptures to His disciples must refer to the Old Testament, as the New was not written when Christ spoke these words. "The inspiration of the Almighty giveth them understanding."— Job xxxii. 8. "The knowledge of the holy is understanding." —Prov. ix. 10. ("Spiritual understanding."—Col. i. 9.) "The Lord giveth wisdom: out of His mouth cometh knowledge and understanding."—Prov. ii. 6. "The words I speak unto you, they are spirit, and they are life."—John vi. 63. Let us become "wayfaring men;" yea, "fools," then ye shall not err.—Is. xxxv. 8. Peter and John were "unlearned and ignorant men," but "they had been with Jesus."—Acts iv. 13.

Ponder over the above verses. "Open thou mine eyes, that I may behold wondrous things out of thy law."—Ps. cxix. 18.

POSSIBLE ANALOGY BETWEEN THE FIRST THREE DAYS OF CREATION AND OUR OWN LIVES.

God creates the world from chaos. Satan defeats His purpose twice by Man, at the Fall and at the Flood. God effects His purpose by *Man* the third time. Thus, as it is with respect to the world, so it is with the Church; it is in bondage in Egypt, and in captivity in Babylon; it is in captivity to Satan, when, by the *Man*, God delivers it for ever. We see the constant repetition of the days of creation in our own lives. We see a distinct scheme continually repeated to this great end. Scripture no longer presents a series of events which are disjointed and unconnected, but we see events intimately connected with the Church collectively, with the world historically, and with man individually. This to me is a great boon, for naturally we are apt to take the Scriptures in their general form to be picked at, and as describing events which are not interwoven with one another. I have only drawn up the repetitions to the end of the Old Testament, taking Pentecost and the Second Coming from the New Testament, but the repetitions occur in the life of our Lord and in the history of the Church and the world from Anno Domini to A.D. 2000.

Of this I have no doubt; and if we studied well by God the Holy Ghost the events of each repetition in the Old Testament, we would be shown by the same Spirit the *things to come*.

The series of events, the repetitions, are thus :—

1. A state of *chaos* or *scattering*—Good mixed up with, and captive to, evil; light mixed up with, and captive to, darkness.

2. A state of light—Good and evil made manifest; light and darkness made manifest.

3. A division—Light separated from darkness; good separated from evil.

4. A gathering — Good gathered, evil destroyed; light gathered, darkness destroyed.

Unless this series of events is understood, the remarks which follow are incomprehensible. The alphabet to study is the creation in Gen. i. 1-20. The earth being surrounded by darkness and swaddled by the deep, the series of events are repeated.

The series 1, 2, 3, 4, tell the great end, when darkness, or evil, finally disappears,— the great gathering, in the typical series of events, *up to the final gathering.* No. 1, which follows No. 4 in the repetitions, does not become *chaos* again, but is more properly a *scattering* of the good among the evil, of light among darkness. The repetitions are like a series of attempts to arrive at a definite point, which are repeated and repeated till that definite point is reached. They are a continual *sifting out*, of *winnowing* good from evil, light from darkness, till the good or light is free from evil or darkness. Evil or darkness cannot be destroyed, till all good or light is winnowed out of it, for if this is not done, and if judgment fell on the darkness or evil, some light or good would be destroyed with the darkness or evil.

In the world historically, the *scattering* of light in the darkness, of good in evil, after a temporary *gathering* together of light or good, is an invasion of the kingdom of evil or darkness, and a winnowing of any good or light that may be in evil or darkness; so that, however painful it is for good or light to be thus *scattered* again among darkness or evil, it is an eventual gainer by such *scattering*, while darkness or evil, though for the moment victorious, is eventually a loser by this invasion.

In man individually, we can see this in ourselves. Take an example such as when we have no changes; we are settled on our lees; we are prosperous, but evil is in us; we are in London, where no call for self-denial directly affects us; all of a sudden we commit some most unmistakable act of selfishness, and we are heartbroken, and all our self-confidence gone; we are *scattered*. Evil has distinctly manifested itself. *Light* has come, showing us ourselves. We have our attention directed to our selfishness. We make an effort, and separate ourselves from it. A *division* takes place in us, and we are no longer selfish in that form; and we are *gathered* together and regain our confidence in ourselves. We settle again on our lees; we have no changes; we fall into some fearfully spiteful ways, *are scattered*. Those ways are manifested. We see them, and are miserable. *Light comes;* we separate from those spiteful ways. *Division comes;* we *gather* ourselves together, being no longer spiteful, and settle again on our lees, to fall again and be *scattered* under some other form of evil (latent in us, which must be destroyed), to see it, to divide from it, to gather together again, and avoid it; to settle again on our lees, and so on till the final gathering.

This is the history of every man's life, of every day's work of man, of the world, of each nation, of the Church, of every member of the Church, *the threshing floor.*

BAPTISM.

Baptism precedes the Holy Communion; thus its type in Genesis must precede the eating of the tree, and this is what I now wish to trace out.

The sacramental eating of the $\begin{Bmatrix} \text{Body} \\ \text{Bread} \end{Bmatrix}$ and $\begin{Bmatrix} \text{Blood} \\ \text{Wine} \end{Bmatrix}$ is the sustaining and quickening of the new man. It has its outward visible forms and acts. It implies the act of one who is alive.

Baptism is termed regeneration—the being born again. It is the seal of the entry into the Body of Christ—the Church. It is termed a burial and resurrection, the putting off of the body of the flesh (Col. ii. 11, 12).

Look at the events of Genesis—creation, the eating, and death. Look then at the remedial sacraments, Baptism and Holy Communion. They continue man's history. Genesis leaves man dead in trespasses and sins, separated from God, consequently deprived of the Holy Ghost's indwelling presence. Therefore Baptism is the sacrament which calls man to life—raises him, while the Communion of the Lord's Supper keeps him in life.

Man was left in Genesis dead from eating; Baptism raises him from the dead, and Holy Communion gives him of the tree of life.

I would notice that in Baptism is an element—water—a material substance, which is applied to the body of man. In Holy Communion are the elements, bread and wine, which are absorbed by the body of man.

Eating connects the Holy Communion with the tree of knowledge of good and evil.

Water must be the connexion of Baptism with some event prior to the fall, and that event is creation. The history of man is creation, eating, death; resurrection or new creation, or regeneration, eating, and life eternal. So we must examine creation to find the meaning of Baptism. "In the beginning, God created the heavens and earth, and the earth was without form and void, and the Spirit of God moved on the face of the waters."

By the word of God, the earth was called out of the waters. This was the creation, for out of that earth man's body was made, so he may be said to have been called out of the waters by the word of God, through the Holy Ghost.

Now here we have the analogy between this creation, or call to life, and Baptism. The earth was dead, so to say, till called to life. So is man, so to say, till born again. The state of earth, before being called into life, was *dead;* the carnal man is *dead.* The state of the earth before it was called into life was like to the state of man at the end of Genesis iii.

What was done by the Word of God through the Holy Ghost to the earth, without form and void, while covered with the deep and with darkness, has to be done to the carnal man ere he can live. He is called by Christ, worked on by the Spirit, and he recognizes his dead state of sin and darkness, and for an outward sign of such acknowledgment, he is baptized, or is figuratively immersed in water, to denote his return to nothingness in hope of the new creation.

As the earth was once covered with water, and dead, so Baptism covers man figuratively with water, to denote his death, to state publicly that he acknowledges death as his due, and, as the earth emerges in its new creation, so man comes forth from Baptism a new creature, and he can then feed on the tree of life in the Holy Communion.

I do not say that Baptism as a rite does raise a man from death, any more than I would say that the Holy Communion is eternal, life-giving, but to a believer. Baptism is resurrection from death, and the Holy Communion is eternal, life-giving.

Baptism does not make a man a Christian. He who is not a Christian before is not made a Christian by that rite, see Romans iv. 10, 11, where it speaks of circumcision as being the seal of Abraham's being already in covenant. Baptism is the seal of a covenant already entered into, and which covenant is that of faith, or of the indwelling of the Holy Ghost.

As a believer does in the Holy Communion partake of the body and blood of Christ, so a believer is in Baptism raised from the dead, has sin remitted, and does, on his emerging from the water, receive the indwelling of the Holy Ghost in his body (for note that he could not believe unless the Holy Ghost enabled his soul to say that Jesus was the Lord).

What I want to point out is this: (1) In Baptism we have water, an element put on the body. (2) In Holy Communion we have bread and wine taken into the body. (3) That the Holy Communion is typified or analogous to the first eating. (4) That it is most probable that the other Christian sacrament, Baptism, is also analogous to some event mentioned prior to the fall. I have long had an idea given me that John iii. was thus to be read: That a death must come between the natural and the new births. This Nicodemus (verse 4) ignored, yet it seems clear. Nicodemus thought the flesh could be remedied and fit for heaven. He did not see that the natural man is actually dead, being separated from God. Baptism is an open avowal that the natural man is hopelessly bad and dead, and can do no good thing, and it figuratively implies the burial of the natural man and a new creation or resurrection from the dead. Holy Communion shows forth Christ's death. Baptism shows forth man's natural state of death and his resurrection. As regards infant Baptism, the child when born is really dead in God's sight, and the parents, bringing it in faith, receive the promise.

Somehow I think both Baptism and

Holy Communion have very much to do with the body, for the elements in each sacrament are inseparable from the body, the elements in one case being *externally*, in the other, *internally*, applied.

He is not a Jew who is one outwardly, neither is that circumcision, which is outward in the flesh (Rom. ii. 28, 29). And so with Baptism; he is not a Christian because he has been baptized. If an unbaptized believer, shall not his non-Baptism be counted Baptism? There are many passages which show forth the uselessness of Baptism in itself without faith, and from this we can see why, after Baptism, the Holy Ghost is not manifestly given to the baptized.

I cannot help thinking that had the writers on Baptism and Holy Communion studied more Genesis i., ii., and iii., they would have been saved much trouble. I shall be very anxious to know what you and —— think of this. It has troubled me for years to know what Baptism meant, though for some years I had seen that between two births must be a death (John iii.). I expect that as water retains in itself the impurities of things placed or washed in it, so the font retains the guilt of sin. It does not seem as if the Holy Ghost used the water as a vehicle further than as rendering it efficacious to remove sin, for it was when Jesus (who, though He had no sin, was man at His Baptism) rose out of water, that the Holy Ghost descended on Him. God is not bound to Baptism, for John the Baptist was filled with the Holy Ghost from his mother's womb, and Cornelius received the Holy Ghost before Baptism. Believers go into the font, as sons of Adam, and emerge as sons of God.

Respecting omission of Baptism in certain cases.

Cornelius received the Holy Ghost before he was baptized (Acts x. 44). Can any man forbid water? Peter and John went down to Samaria (Acts viii.

15-16). Philip had preached the gospel, and men had been baptized in the name of the Lord Jesus, but they had not received the Holy Ghost till Peter and John laid hands on them.

By these two instances, we see that the Holy Ghost was not given necessarily with Baptism nor was the Holy Ghost withheld because there had been no Baptism. Paul circumcised Timothy (Acts xvii. 3) because of the Jews (1 Cor. vii. 19). Circumcision is nothing, uncircumcision is nothing, but the keeping of the commandments of God. Paul here, because of the Jews, circumcised Timothy. Yet (Gal. ii. 3) he will not circumcise Titus. This exemplifies that he acted with the judgement God gave him. Certainly his circumcising Timothy was a concession to the Jews, whom he, in a way, feared. For if he did not fear them, why did he perform this Judaic rite? I say feared, but mean that he was taught by God to make this concession for wiser purposes and for the avoidance of dissensions. Now I think this would justify the holding in abeyance of Baptism in cases where there is a fanatical population. For Baptism does not make a Christian, any more than circumcision made a Jew. The putting off figuratively of the body of flesh, by the outward Baptism, does no more than the putting off figuratively of the filth of the flesh by outward circumcision. I think we can read 1 Cor. vii., "Art thou called, being a slave, care not for it, but if thou canst be made free, use it rather," together with "Ye are bought with a price;" "Be not servants of men. Ye are free in Christ;" thus: if ye are called to be free in Christ, care not for the outward ceremony. If thou canst obtain it, "use it rather." Baptism is nothing; un-Baptism is nothing, "but faith which worketh by love" (Gal. v. 6), that is, the indwelling of the Holy Ghost —the new creature (Gal. vi. 15).

How quickly Paul acted with respect to

the jailer (Acts xvi. 33). In the same hour of the night, while the jailer was washing their stripes, Paul talked to him and then baptized him. The jailer baptized Paul's stripes; Paul baptized him from his sins. Why in the face of Acts, which is essentially the Mission direction-book, are men so careful? is it because they do not believe themselves? All the household of the jailer was baptized. This was at Philippi, the chief city (Acts xvi. 12), so the prison must have been a big one, and the jailer must have had many in his household. One wonders whether the jailer and his household would have come up to the requirements of the clergy of this day who are Missionaries.

What did we lose by the first eating? (I do not like the word "fall," it is not scriptural.) We lost the Holy Ghost. What did we gain by the second eating? (Either spiritually or actually we must feed on Christ.) We gained the Holy

Ghost. Think over that, for it is very important.

The loss of the Holy Ghost is separation from God—death—so we are naturally dead in God's sight, and when we are immersed in the font, we figuratively own it by our burial in the water.

Adam, the first man, came out of the water in the first creation. He sinned; we were in him and all died in him, so we are all dead in Christ's sight. We are then all in a place common to all—the grave, the place of the dead. We acknowledge that when we enter the waters of the font, we are as Adam was. We rise out of the font in the new creation, in the new Adam, Christ. In Him, we are no longer dead. We live. Our emerging from the font is resurrection, and in Him we receive (what we had previously lost) the Holy Ghost, which is our life.

In Adam all men are created, die, return to the dust, go into one receptacle out of which they came. What is the gathering place of all men?—the grave. Christ, the second Adam, gathers us together, from that grave in Himself, the new creation. When we go into the font we typify our state, and by so entering the figurative grave of waters, we can be gathered together in the new man, Christ (*synagogue* is the word used for the gathering together of waters in Septuagint, and also, John xi. 52, "gather the children of God which are scattered abroad"). Baptism figuratively says we go back to Genesis i. as we enter the font, and we rise out of it in the new Adam, Christ. We feed on the tree of life. We rise, as it were, in Revelation xxii., where there is the river, the tree of life, God, and the Lamb.

Before the Holy Ghost is *renewed* (mark that word, for it shows man once possessed Him and then lost Him), man must enter the figurative grave, must acknowledge his death and hopeless state. For as the anointing oil cannot be put on the flesh, neither can the carnal receive the Holy Ghost. The fleshly mind is enmity, cannot receive the Holy Ghost (Rom. viii. 9, a very strong verse).

Baptism is the sowing of the natural body in expectation of the raising of the spiritual body. By Baptism we own to the necessity of such sowing. We own our natural state as only fit to be sown or buried.

The first man, Adam, was made a living soul and died, and figuratively, in baptism, is buried. The second or last Adam, Christ, is the quickening spirit (the Lord from heaven) which raises from the dead.

Baptism is owing to corruption.
Baptism is owing to dishonour.
Baptism is owing to weakness.

(1 Cor. xv.)

This shows us that Baptism is no unimportant matter. For true Baptism of infants agreeing by sponsors who are believers, or when accepted by adults, is virtually the acknowledgment of the flesh being able to do no good thing. Also this view respecting Baptism would seem strongly to support the baptizing of infants. For it signifies the burial of a dead thing which cannot move of itself. A babe is dead as far as its will, etc., is concerned, and when it is figuratively buried in Baptism by believers, there is reason to suppose—indeed our faith in God obliges us to believe—that it will rise in Christ.

I think, in Baptism, the adult who wishes to be free of his carnal nature, and who believes in Jesus and is baptized, does receive the Holy Ghost in his *body*. The elements, in one case, by which he obtains the benefit to his *body*, being bread and wine, the elements, by which he puts off the *body* of his flesh in the other, being the water. The elements in both sacraments are material, and both are sanctified to the body by the Holy Ghost, one for sustenance of life in Christ, the other for resurrection from the dead in Christ, the new Adam.

Was not the eating of the forbidden fruit a disruption of the union with God, and from that the formation of an union with Satan? If we examine the word faith, it is the property derived directly from the presence of the Holy Ghost, for "none can say Jesus is the Lord, but by the Holy Ghost," and in many other passages this is shown forth. Faith is the direct effect of the indwelling of the Holy Ghost. There can be no faith where the Holy Ghost is not indwelling. Any one saying that he possesses belief in our Lord, and denying the indwelling of the Holy Ghost in him, is a liar and does not believe; or he makes God a liar.

Thence I conclude, that every word, deed, thought, done without union with Christ by the Holy Ghost is exactly the eating of the forbidden fruit. Hence also, that every word, deed, thought, done in union with Christ by the Holy Ghost, is exactly the eating of the tree of life.

That, as the eating of forbidden fruit can be thus accomplished by word or thought, as well as by deed, yet as the deed in the past instance was the apex of this act, so the eating of the tree of life —CHRIST—can be accomplished by word or thought, but is essentially accomplished by deed. The union in Christ by the indwelling of the Holy Ghost is the Alpha and Omega of all life, and this view commends itself to our reason. The outcome of this union is a fruit. It needs no effort; if we seek and nourish the union, the fruits of the Holy Ghost cannot but follow as sequences.

There can be no life or union with Christ, but by the Holy Ghost. Redemption, or the benefits of our Lord's expiation, cannot be grasped or be beneficial to any one, except by the indwelling of the Holy Ghost; "If any man have not the spirit of Christ, he is none of His" (Rom. viii. 9). If he hath not that which maketh the union, he cannot be united to

Christ. That the descent of the Holy Ghost was consequent on our Lord's suffering is evident; He could not descend till Christ ascended. On Christ's ascension, He descends.

To many it would be an ineffable blessing to know that the only way to be holy or like Christ is by seeking and nourishing the Holy Ghost's presence in us. As for the sequences, to deny that they will follow, is to deny the Godhead of the Holy Ghost. When I think of what a long wilderness journey I have had, how I have tried, in vain, to patch up matters, I cannot say too much on this subject. Speaking as a man, what a great blessing it would have been for some one to have said to me (though it is clear in the Scriptures), "Seek the realization of the Holy Ghost's presence in you, and leave the rest." No argument is wanted, just these words only. Believers in Christ have God the Holy Ghost living in them. The nourishing of this truth in daily life is all that is needed, and He feeds us by His Scriptures. All the rest follows as sequences.

Connexion between the Fall of Man and Holy Communion.

In a Jewish class book for the young I found the Fall omitted, and on speaking to ———, a Jewish clergyman, he said the Jews do not recognise it as a reality, but date their disorders from the making of the calf. One can understand that, for they think that they can justify themselves by the law, and also by making the calf the reason of their Fall, they keep the Fall certainly to themselves as a nation.

I am going to work out the Fall for you.

" Tree of knowledge of good and evil"—tree of learning what is to be known of good and evil. By eating of this tree man became as God, for God said, " Behold man is become as one of us, to know good and evil," where "become" is from the Hebrew, "to experience the same as," "to become like," to be "made." This is remarkable, for it would imply that though man was made in the likeness and image of God, the faculty of knowing evil, though it must have been present, was not developed in him before his eating. Angels and devils could never be said to have become like "one of us."

Note that the prohibition respecting the tree was given before woman was builded of the rib; also that woman was builded in the garden, man was made out of it. Man was driven out, woman is not mentioned. To woman no reason was given; to man God said, " Because thou hast eaten." The penalty of eating, " Dying, thou shalt die," must be compared with the sentences, "because thou hast eaten," " cursed is the ground," "till thou return to the ground, for out of it wast thou taken, for dust thou art, to dust thou shalt return." Septuagint has, as penalty, "die by death." "The woman saw it was good for food, pleasant to the eye, and a tree desired to make one wise." Septuagint has, for the last paragraph, "beautiful to contemplate." Wordsworth quotes other authorities to the same effect.

Eph. ii. 2, " Prince of the power of the air, the spirit that now worketh in the children of disobedience." Therefore the prince of the power of the air, or Satan, does work in the children of disobedience, and it is evident that he began to work in man, when man disobeyed God by eating the forbidden fruit.

We may suppose that if all things were permissible to man with this exception, that this exception was made because it would be hurtful to man. Had Eve never eaten what was forbidden, she never could have been worked in by the spirit of disobedience, Satan; and, look at it as you will, the reflection must strike us that by the fact of her eating she admitted Satan to enter and work in her.

1 Cor. x. 20, clearly shows that the sacrificing to idols is synonymous to fellowship with devils ("the things which the Gentiles sacrifice, they sacrifice to devils, and not to God, and I would not that ye should have fellowship with devils").

The cup of blessing is the communion or participation of the blood of Christ. The bread we break is the communion or participation of the body of Christ (1 Cor. x. 16).

The drinking of the cup is the becoming partaker of the Lord's table; the drinking of the cup of devils is the becoming partaker of the table of devils. Throughout this chapter, there is the parallelism of two eatings, two sacrifices, two sequences of such eating—that is, participation, two fellowships, two communions, from which stand out the facts of two eatings and the sequences of such eatings, namely, communion with the power eaten with, which communion signifies participation in the attributes of such power.

However we may explain away the term, St. John (vi. 56) states the indwelling of Christ in those who eat His flesh and drink His blood, and (vi. 53) states as clearly that, except we do so, there is no life in us. Therefore, it would seem clear that this eating implies Christ's indwelling, and 1 Cor. x. certainly implies that to those who sacrifice (or which have fellowship—verse 20, where they are synonymous terms) with devils have also the mutual indwelling with devils. Now, there can be no doubt but that Eve's eating of the forbidden tree was a fellowship with Satan first, because Satan was with her; secondly, because it was not in fellowship with God; thirdly, because it was with the spirit of disobedience. In regarding this question, it is well to keep clear of all the sacrifices of the Mosaic dispensation, and to keep before us the Fall and the Restoration, of which the prominent point is that Sacrament by which we show forth the Lord's death till He come. I say this because I cannot see how Eve sacrificed to Satan, though I see that she had fellowship, participation, communion with him.

If the prince of the power of the air works in the children of disobedience, he must at one time have worked in every one, for all have sinned, and he must have worked at some definite period subsequent to the creation of man, and it is manifest that he did so when Eve disobeyed. Therefore, it is thus that he worked in her, and he worked in her because she ate of the forbidden fruit. There is no necessity to think that he was the fruit, but he was in the fruit.

Take the mode of acceptance of the Body and Blood of our Lord. We believe that the bread and wine, through God's ordination, are instrumentally the cause of mystical participation with Christ, by which He becomes wholly ours, and we become

His as closely as His flesh is His body, and His blood is His blood. And it is by the bread and wine that that cementing union is accomplished, by eating and drinking His body and His blood, by the actual fact of so eating. Now here we do not believe that the bread becomes flesh, or the wine blood, neither do I suppose that the fruit was changed; but I think there can be no doubt but that there was a real spiritual entry of Satan into Eve's body by the fact of her eating.

(Numbers ix. 13, any one neglecting to keep the passover was cut off. Exodus xiii. 8, " Thou shalt shew thy son that day," the reason of the Passover, viz., redemption from Egypt, death of the first born. Paul's word " show forth his death " is connected with this verse. The Jews called it the Hagadah, or showing forth, when they reserved a portion of the unleavened bread, and when the children asked why they did it, the head of the family replied :—" This is the bread of affliction which our fathers ate in the land of affliction ; let him that is hungry come and eat of this Passover, for it is our refuge and saviour.)

I think it is established that the prince of the power of the air entered us and worked in the children of disobedience by the fact of Eve's eating the forbidden fruit. She was out of communion with God, and lost the presence of the Holy Ghost, by whom we have communion. This is implied by the Restoration in Christ when He restored to us that union which is by the Holy Ghost, the promise of my Father the earnest of inheritance. From the passage, Rom. viii. 11, the spirit of Him who raised Christ from the dead shall quicken your mortal bodies by His Spirit which dwelleth in you. I would think that the Holy Spirit is in union with the soul, in the first place, and that He then, by the quickened soul, quickens the mortal body. As the Holy Ghost can only work on the soul, which is spiritual, in a spiritual manner (and, one may say, irrespective of the body), how is it that that body, which by an actual fact (that of eating) fell under the power of evil, can be reached? and though I put this with all diffidence, I think that it is reasonable, and also scriptural, to think that it is reached by the same medicine as that by which it fell and allowed the entry of Satan—that is, by eating.

There is a close connexion between the Sacrament of the Lord's Supper and the resurrection of the body. "Whosoever eateth My flesh, and drinketh My blood, I will raise him up at the last day." —St. John vi. 54. And we feel this— that if we actually participate worthily in His Sacrament, we do, by spiritually eating that bread and drinking that wine, receive His body into our bodies, and His blood into our blood, cleansing us wholly ; and is it possible to think that these bodies can ever perish after such an intimate union with the Godhead, as the eating and drinking of His body and blood implies?

We have to think that the body was pre-eminently active in the Fall, by its actual absorption of what was forbidden; and here, in this second eating, it is also pre-eminently active in the same way. In the first eating, the body offered up the soul (for the soul could not care whether it ate or not); in the second eating, the soul offers the body up as a sacrifice. In the first eating, the body ruled; in the second eating, the soul rules.

In speaking of Eve so often, I mean Adam as well.

Why are we all so dead? Why is not our flesh quickened? Really, I think that many, many are really good, earnest, Christians. Why are they so morose? They realise God's mercy in Christ, but they are tied to a corpse—their body. All will be well with them, but as yet they have no happiness. Why drag this corpse about? It emits the odours of corruption; it is heavy and troublesome. Why not quicken it? Truly, I believe it is because the Holy Communion is so much neglected. Though it is a corpse, it can still eat; and if the soul is alive, and quickened by the Holy Ghost, why should not the soul take the body to where it can absorb the body and blood of Christ, the result of which must be life. It may be languid at first, probably more corruption may be thrown out; but it will soon live, and its life is for ever. It will never see death; it will the resurrection of life.

A——, in Mauritius, wrote to me the other day: "I have much to put up with, and get snubs enough, but I have kept to the eating, and I do not care for them now." He was not what you call religious, but he was struck by the analogy, and ate, and lives for ever. What is wanted in order to eat? If we fence any tree, fence the tree of knowledge of good and evil, for it is still here. Do not let us fence the tree of life. God gives us the way to it in Christ. All that is needed is, "I am ill; I wish I were well; I hate and abhor myself; I have faint hopes of deriving any benefit: but I will trust Him, and do, in remembrance of Him, what He bade me do." Can one doubt of the result? Sum it up. All that is required is—first, illness; secondly, the wish to be well; thirdly, obedience to His word.

I think many, many would agree to the first and the second. Why not agree to the third? It is such a little thing; the benefits are so infinite. If any doubt it, look at the forbidden fruit; it was such a little offence, yet look at its results, needing the Almighty God to take flesh and to suffer agonies, to do away with its effects.

THOU SHALT NOT EAT. TAKE, EAT.

What efforts have been made for the cure of bodily ailments, what sums have been expended. What diagnoses of diseases have been made, yet, at the best the remedies can only retard for a short time the certain inevitable finale. Surely, if such pains have been taken in inquiries into physical sickness, it is worth much more to inquire into the causes and remedy of man's moral sickness, for no man doubts but that he is morally sick, that he is not in his normal state.

As the story is told of the fall, it seems weak in comparison to the immense evils the fall produced. The temptation seems trivial; yet if examined, was it trivial? Eve was adamant against any desires for honours — carriages, horses, jewels, fine clothes; these things would not tempt her curiosity. But animal desire to eat could do so.

Given a palace, with injunction to occupy and explore the whole, and prohibition to open one particular cupboard, under the penalty of something unknown, a penalty which could not appear to the ignorant to be very deterrent, the wish would be to open that cupboard. Place before a child 999 lozenges and prohibit the eating of one, and the child will yearn after that one. And so with Eve; the name and prohibition to eat of the tree of *knowledge* was a very great temptation, it was such an apparently trivial act, that no great harm could arise from eating of it. And we know the dire sequence. Let your ingenuity be exercised to find out some other more suitable test of Eve's fidelity to her Maker; it will not be easy. She ate in *trust in herself*, and *in distrust of God;* she ate, after reasoning for herself. She *was* in *union with God*, and she *broke away* from her union.

The trees were *sacramental* trees, mystic trees, natural trees, endued for a time with mystic properties (sacrament means set apart). In eating of the forbidden tree Eve *trusted in herself, distrusted God*, and *communed with Satan* (to commune is to have attributes in common with one of the two communing parties). Thus by communing in disobedience to God's command, Eve naturally *communed with Satan*, for there are only two powers, that of good, and that of evil; and as Eve broke her communion with God by her disobedience, she necessarily communed with Satan and acquired *his attributes of evil*, viz., she was poisoned by evil introduced into her actual body by the eating of a substance which, naturally good (all the trees were blessed), was to her endued with evil, inasmuch as it was forbidden to her by God.

Men may say that it is absurd to think that the fact of eating a fruit could have caused such vast effects to the whole human race, but it must be considered that in Eve were all mankind, and thus if her body did eat, and assimilate a substance forbidden, and consequently evil, so did those her children do the same, for the poison would affect every portion of her body; the fruit was the *vehicle* of the virus of evil. I thereupon say distinctly, that the moral poisoning man acquired was from the actual eating of a fruit which was forbidden, that this fruit was the cause of the poisoning, that had it not been eaten, the poisoning would never have taken place; also that it was the body of man which was poisoned, and not the soul, which, however, became dormant, or dead, owing to its oneness with the body; and on which body the sentence of death was pronounced: "In the day thou eatest thereof thou shalt surely die." That the body was the offender, that the body was tainted, can be seen by the sentence "For dust thou art, unto dust shalt thou return, for out of the ground wast thou taken," which could not be said of the soul which was breathed into man by God, and which was therefore divine.

Men may say that the sentence or penalty in this disobedience was too heavy considering tne offence; but what was the offence? It was the wilful breaking away of Eve from God;

she avowed preference of herself to Him. If one man is in covenant with another, and the terms of that covenant are mutual support, and if that other breaks, for his selfish ends, that contract for some wretched selfish purpose, the principle cannot be considered hard in cancelling that contract, the more so as the selfish purpose is carried out in communion with his enemy, and that by this selfish purpose his late co-partner is tainted and made unfit for his company. So it is with man in covenant with God; he breaks the covenant in communion with Satan, becomes tainted, and communion between God and man ceases.

It is necessary to bear in mind that the cessation of man's communion with God is the cause of man's misery, and that the evil of this world is the result of the absence of God and presence of Satan. It is not, so to speak, a sentence; it is the *sequel* of *God's absence*, it is dark because light is absent. If there is no light, there must be darkness; if God is not, Satan must be. I consider this very wonderful.

God framed man of the dust of the ground (shaped him as a potter shapes clay; He framed the animal man) and breathed into his nostrils the breath of life—two processes. He took dust of the earth, the *devil's earth* (for the devil said it was his; he is the prince of it), and breathed His own substance into it; consequently man is made up of a divine essence of God and a body of Satan's earth. Hence it is that the combat of this life between the soul and Satan is for the body. Satan disputed for the body of Moses; it was his, for it was made of his earth. To redeem the body is our great hope, and its redemption is the earnest or "arles" of a far greater victory over him, hereafter: it is the test case.

I have, I think, established the poisoning of mankind. I will try and explain my belief respecting the antidote.

In nature, if a poison is taken into the body, in which it spreads its virus, to neutralise it an antidote must be taken into the same body, in which it must spread its healing effects.

In nature, man does not trouble himself, if poisoned, as to how, and in what way, the antidote will work; he may not know how it may work; nor how the poison he suffers from has worked; it is enough for him that he suffers and wishes his cure. He takes the antidote in trust, just as he may have taken the poison in trust, for, as a rule, he does not try and poison himself. Man never seeks evil for itself; he seeks good in evil. Thus it suffices to man to know he is morally poisoned in order that he may desire his cure and be healed.

Now, analogous to the *Thou shalt not eat*—the words God spake to man at the first—are almost the last words of Christ to His disciples, and through them to the world, *Take, eat, this is my body.*

Here, then, is an actual substance (bread) to be eaten, taken into the poisoned body, assimilated with it, and which actual substance is *bidden* to be eaten by Christ, and is the vehicle or conduit by which Christ imparts His Divine attributes to that poisoned body; just as much as the *forbidden* fruit was the vehicle or conduit by which Satan imparted his evil attributes to that body and poisoned it.

Man ate in utter ignorance of the sequel in the case of the forbidden fruit, for death was not then known; so man may eat in utter ignorance of the sequel in the case of the sacramental bread.

In the first case he ate in trust in self distrust in God, and communion with Satan.

In the second case he eats in trust in God, distrust in self, and communion with God.

To the world, both eatings are foolishness, yet they are the wisdom of God.

Man never seeks evil for itself, he seeks

good out of evil. Eve sought good out of the forbidden fruit, but she sought it in trust in herself and distrust in God.

A babe can understand if it is ill that it needs remedies, and will take nauseous ones, in trust, from the mother. Man can therefore understand the sacramental antidote, when once he knows his moral poisoning, yet the highest intellect cannot fathom the depths of either the first sacrament with Satan, or the last sacrament with Christ.

I say, then, *What is needed of a man to eat the sacrament?* Simply a sense that he is morally sick, and wishes to be better—and few men do not feel both these sentiments.

Why is it that the sacramental antidote is so neglected? Because it is so simple, it seems to the world nonsense; yet "is the table of the Lord contemptible?"

We may add to this question of Malachi, Is not the Sacrament of the Lord's Supper the only rite which will exist in the future ages (Luke xxii. 18) ? It is essentially the wedding feast of the Church; it is the outward pledge of the mutual indwelling of man in God, and God in man.

The Human Tongue.

In eating, the first member of sensation of the body is the tongue. It is the first member touched.

The tongue is a fire, a world of iniquity; it defileth the whole body, and setteth on fire the whole of nature, and it is set on fire by hell. Everything has been tamed, but the tongue no man can tame; it is an unruly evil, full of deadly poison, with which we bless God and curse men, who are His image, thereby implying it is used by God, and also by Satan, for we could not bless God but by God's working, nor could we curse men but by Satan's will, which is ours by nature.

The tongue was given man to express

his thoughts and conceptions. Who whet their tongue like a sword, and bend their bow to shoot their arrows, even bitter words; their tongue is a sharp razor. Death and life are in the power of the tongue. Whoso keepeth his tongue keepeth his soul from death; they bend their tongue like their bow for lies; their tongue is as an arrow shot out. Of the new man it is the glory, viz., respecting leaving his soul in hell (Psalm xvi. 9, and Acts ii. 26), where glory is represented by the tongue. The tongue is the instrument of lies, of treachery, of slander, of blasphemy, of spite, of malice, of unclean speaking, in fact of all iniquity, to the Satanic and carnal; and the day of Pentecost, with the descent of the tongues of fire, showed that it was the king of evil of the body. He that seemeth to be religious and bridleth not his tongue, that man's religion is in vain, he deceiveth his own heart. Our Lord says He will give us a tongue, or mouth, to repel adversaries. Evidently, from the Scriptures, the tongue is a king, either for evil or for good. As in nature, so in spiritual things, the tongue shows the internal state. Out of the abundance of the heart the mouth or tongue speaketh. In His mouth was no guile. We came from the mouth of God. He breathed the breath of lives—the Word of God. He laid the coal on the mouth of Isaiah, the coal from off the altar.

Taken thus, comparing things seen with things unseen, how appropriate that the tongue which first touched the forbidden fruit, and acquired its evil, should be the first member to take the bidden fruit, the bread and wine. Is it not to us a great prevention against evil speaking to communicate worthily? and we cannot think it possible ever to communicate worthily if we never communicate at all. We must in ourselves ever be unworthy, but it is by communicating in obedience that we are given the power to communicate worthily. What is it if, in our trial of communing, we may have fleshly troubles. Christ never invited us to His table to hurt us. He invites us to heal us, to feed us. Let a man communicate feebly, with little ecstasy, or perhaps with only a feeble wish to be better, he may be smitten in his flesh, to better him in some way. But it is possible for men to communicate worthily, though this is not possible while they continue their fearfully treacherous words against one another. I speak of the common parlance of life, where we all are so apt to err. We could not keep repeating that unkind, amusing story, of X or Y. If we were often communing, it would choke us.

Therefore there is a close analogy in the remedy and the sickness, as shown by the tongue. We can tell how we are progressing by the tongue far quicker than by any other way. It is a sure barometer of the heart, and it is one we can see, and others see at once. We become very stupid to the world, but poor wounded souls come to us; they know that he who keeps his tongue will not plant bitter words like barbed stings in their wounds. Christ is the corner of defence to that man. " Forasmuch as ye did it to them, ye did it to Me." The tongue is glib, serpent-like, and it is odd that women have it in such perfection, which none have ever doubted. It is their defence. The woman ate first, and the tongue is her particular forte. Yet when women speak good, how well they speak out. They are in this point the salt of the earth. The tongue sits on the four-horned throne, a sort of crown—compare the incense altar. Prayer is the incense before the throne of God, but the tongue is the sacrifice of the altar, and it must be quickened by the fire of God, not by the fire of hell. I think all the troubles of the Church have come from the callous way in which we treat the Communion. No one can doubt but that its constant celebration and faithful reception must tend towards unity. We are members one of another. We are brothers even to —— ; query, may it not be our remissness which created ——, so to say? If the Holy Ghost spoke through us as He would through many (if the pipe of their bodies were in harmony, that is, if it were sanctified), would not the voice be God's voice? Again, why is it we have the Holy Ghost spoken of as "it"? Either such an expression argues that the speaker does not know the Holy Ghost, or else he so little regards Him, that it matters little how He is termed, yet probably that man would claim, and perhaps rightly, that his body was the temple of the Holy Ghost. When our Lord appeared at Emmaus, He broke bread, and they knew Him. When He ascended, He and His disciples had been eating together. The Day of Pentecost they had been eating, for they were accused of being full of new wine. To me these were celebrations of the Communion.

This Jesus hath God raised up ; therefore being at the right hand of God, and having received of the Father the promise of the Holy Ghost, He hath shed forth this, these gifts to us.

FRUIT.

Fruit is the result of an union between two.

Work is the result of one, governing or ruling another.

Fruits of the spirit imply an agreement between the Holy Spirit and the spirit of man; they (these fruits) are the result of that agreement.

Fruits can only be produced when the two, by whose union they are produced, work together.

Works of the flesh imply the rule of evil, or of the world, over the, for a time subordinated, faculties of man.

Works can be performed by one superior through an inferior, either by that superior ruling the inferior, or by the inertness of the inferior, or in accordance with the spirit of that inferior.

Works are rewarded with wages, namely what is earned.

Fruits are results, are increase, and imply continuation in the same line.

No good tree can produce evil fruit, for it can only produce fruit at all by its union with one of its own kind, which would be good.

No evil tree can produce good fruit, for the same reason.

Fungus can be produced by the working of an extraneous cause on a good tree, but it is not fruit.

Therefore it is that the fruits of holiness can never be produced by the action of man of himself; they are the result of his union with the Holy Spirit. Man is bound to be sterile without this union; all the efforts he makes are nothing more than abortive, unimpregnated buds; hence all efforts to produce holiness, made by man, from any motive of self, must be sterile. The spirit of those efforts is not the fecundating spirit, by which they alone become fertile. When efforts are made *not* from motives of self, then, as the same spirit exists, the fecundating spirit, these efforts become fruits, they are fecundated. By their fruits ye shall know them.

Dying Thou shalt Die.

We live when our bodies perform their functions; we die when they cease to perform their functions.

Each of us is endowed at birth with a body which is capable of passing through a *series* of *changes;* when *these changes* or developments *cease*, or are gone through, we die.

These changes or developments are ever going on in us, even as the sand runs from an hour-glass, and are one continuous disintegration, oxidisation, and burning of the constituent parts of the body—their death in fact.

This death of the constituent parts of the body, perpetually taking place in all parts of the body, keeps up the life of the body till a time comes when these deaths no longer possess a recuperative power, and life becomes extinct, the sand has run out.

Up to a certain time these deaths give life to other constituent parts; when they cease to do so, we die. Our body therefore is continually "*dying, till we die.*"

The deaths are caused by oxygen, which we obtain by *breathing*.

When man was first shaped, his organs were all complete, but lifeless; when God breathed into his nostrils, he lived. Had he continued in union with God, we may suppose he would have lived for ever, that the breath of his life would have been sustained, but when he fell and broke his union with God, dying he dies, for then the time comes that his body loses the entire effect of God's breath. His life, in one case, was an hour-glass with an infinite quantity of sand, in the other, as an hour-glass with a fixed modicum of sand.

Truly that view of the Holy Ghost as the breath of God is very wonderful; it startles at first, I own, but when the Scripture is considered, it supports the view. God the Father, God the Son, God the Holy Ghost; three persons in one God, co-equal, co-eternal. Read the Athanasian Creed. *God the Father*, neither created nor begotten; *God the Son*, of the Father alone, not made nor created, but *begotten; God the Holy Ghost*, of the Father and of the Son, neither made, nor created, nor begotten, but *proceeding*. From Christ's side proceeded forth blood and water, the Sacraments of His Church.

Considering what I have said about the very great work of the Holy Ghost, it is wonderful that, when at the end, God the

Father is seen, the Lamb is seen, and the Lamb's Bride is seen. Where is the Holy Ghost, who purifies, sanctifies, and is the Life of the Bride? It is by Him (the Holy Ghost) *the Lamb's Bride is one with the Lamb.* This unity is her sole life.

I feel now quite satisfied about this matter, and I account for the same not being seen by others (*i.e.* not being shown to them by the Holy Ghost), by people not reading the Scriptures. There is the root of all ignorance. It is quite impossible for man to know God but by the Holy Ghost's tuition, by His own written Word, which He, the Holy Ghost, wrote Himself, though He spoke through the lips of the prophets.

Let us consider this question again. It is accepted by us that God the Son took man's nature, and is *man* (infinitely great is *that* condescension, yet He did so, and also condescended in suffering for our foul offences). What God the Son did is not derogatory to God the Holy Ghost to do. And we have the Scripture to say He lives in our bodies. "Know ye not that your body is the Temple of the Holy Ghost?" Christ, God the Son, assumed human nature to Himself, not for a time, but for *eternity*, never to be put off.

He is the God-man for ever and ever. He changeth not. The Holy Ghost dwells in each member of Christ, in each individual of the Church. We have that clear promise, for no one would be a member of Christ, or an individual of the Church, if the cause of that union was absent—*i.e.* God the Holy Ghost. We cannot believe that the Holy Ghost can willingly leave the members of Christ's body, or the individual of the Church, for His leaving implies a cessation of the union between them and Christ, He being the cause of that union. So we may safely conclude that the Holy Ghost wills to dwell in the members of Christ, consequently the Holy Ghost is—

dare we say it?—*incarnated* in each member of Christ, each individual of the Church. And thus we see that in The Revelation there is God the Father; God the Son, incarnated in Christ Jesus; and God the Holy Ghost, incarnated in the Bride of Christ Jesus.

Salvation comes through the Awakening of the Dormant Soul.

If a man is troubled or weary he tries to find out the reason of such uneasiness. We feel hot, and detect that we are uncomfortable by the heat; we try and get cool and *vice versâ*. This we do naturally, and the same is the case with us respecting the attacks evil makes upon us. By what gate does Satan enter? How does he work in us? What is our true *We?* What is the true spirit? What is the power of Satan? All these are most important points to study, for they affect our peace. Nothing is so dangerous to us as an insidious foe, and thus it is worth while to study where that insidious foe lurks. Nothing Satan likes better than to creep in quietly, not to be detected. Suppose a captain of a hundred men, of which one hundred some ten are traitors; they leaven the rest. A good captain would feel that something was wrong with his hundred men, and he would seek much to find out the cause. When once he detected the traitors he would be comforted and take his measures accordingly. The power of Satan is from his insidious friends in us. Our Lord's temptations came direct from Satan externally, for, being sinless, Satan had no inward allies in our Lord—thence our Lord's words (John xiv. 30) that Satan had nothing in Him. Let us first think where the seat of our troubles lies, for in that seat we shall find the traitors who are friendly with Satan, and by whom he works. At once we can answer that it is the *body*. Agreeing with that, is the fact that the body ate the fruit, and on the body came the sentence to return to the dust, and it is supported by the verse, " He that is dead ceaseth from sin." We therefore agree that the body is the seat of the traitors. We are made up of soul and body, and as long as they keep together we live. If you make a hole in the heart, out of it flies the soul at once, leaving the body as dust, and therefore free from sin, or Satan's influence. For, powerful as Satan is, he cannot vivify the body. The soul, therefore, is the vivifying power of the body. "Let not sin reign in your mortal bodies, that you should obey the lusts thereof" (Rom. vi. 12). This would imply that Satan is inclined to reign in those bodies, and the Scripture goes on to speak of the yielding our members, as weapons, or servants, or instruments, by which Satan works. Before the Fall the soul governed the body and used its members as it willed. By the Fall and the eating, Satan entered the body, and he usurped the soul's functions and used the members of the body as weapons, servants, instruments, unto iniquity. The soul, being dead, had no power. So I think that a carnal man has a dormant soul, and therefore he has Satan usurping the dormant soul's functions and using the body as he wills. When the Holy Ghost awakens the soul, then begins the contest between it and Satan for the rule of the body. St. James (iv. 1) gives the reason of the struggle and disquietude in believers—lust warring in our members. In 1 Peter ii. 11, the same warfare is said to be against the *soul*. We therefore can see that the evil desires we have, are, in believers, the work truly of Satan and *exterior* to us. At the same time, the corrupt tendencies of our bodies afford Satan aid (James i. 15). If we consider that the corrupt tendencies of the body are the sole advantage that Satan has (for, if those corrupt tendencies—which come from the first eating—did not exist, we would be as our Lord, that is, Satan would have nothing in us), how important it is to study how we should destroy those corrupt tendencies. Who are the traitors in us? As they came by eating, what more natural than that they should be destroyed by eating, spiritually and actually, Christ who is the Life. I think our life is one progressive series of finding out Satan. As we grow in grace, we are constantly finding out that he is a traitor; he is continually being unmasked. If we look at our past life, we can see that a few years ago we should not have given a thought about saying things which now we cannot say without a twinge of conscience.

This view has comforted me, for I did not like to think the soul a sinner, except by imputation, as being one with the body. James and Peter evidently say the attack of Satan is against the soul, and from the vantage ground of the body. Satan would give nothing for the body without the soul, for it would be dust, his portion. This somewhat explains the subjection of the creature unto vanity in Romans viii.

The body is the sinner, and the soul sins by imputation, being one with it. This also shows that Satan does virtually possess the carnal man, which we were all once, and he uses the body as his own. The soul being dormant, can do nothing till the Holy Ghost raises it. All this is supported by the views expressed in Scripture of the devil wandering about looking for an habitation, having lost his first estate and left his own habitation, seeking strange flesh (Jude 7). Note this. Because the soul died or became dormant by separation from the Holy Ghost, at the first eating, it is not therefore absent from the body, and it consequently gives the body life in its members. The expression *dies*, applied to the soul, is scarcely correct, for it never dies; it is dormant. While it is present with the body, the body lives; when the soul leaves the body, the body falls to dust. The leaving of the body by the soul is *death*.

The New Birth.

It certainly was one of the most important matters concerning man which led Nicodemus to come to Christ, and led to His stating, "that unless a man be born again, he cannot see the kingdom of God." There is much haziness as to this new birth, whether it is an entirely new formation, or whether it is the Resurrection, or a resuscitation of an existing formation; whether it is a revivifying or reanimating of a pre-existence, or whether it is a new creation, never having had a previous existence.

A man to be *born again* must have been *born already*. This seems implied by Nicodemus's question, whether it was probable for a man born once to be born a second time? Christ does not directly answer this query, but He implies that a death intervenes between the first and second birth in the remark that man must be born of water, the type of the grave or resting place of the dead.

If the new birth is a new creation never possessed of a pre-existence, then it must be assumed that a babe is born deficient of some creation, which may or may not be given to that babe by God at some period posterior to its earthly birth.

Such a supposition would imply two sets of human beings, one set with, the other set without, this new creation.

Now Scripture states this new birth to be a quickening of the dead (Eph. ii. 1), a reviving, a resurrection of something which has died, and therefore I am inclined to think that the new birth is the arousing of a dormant pre-existence—the rising from, as it were, a grave—of an existence which had died, and that every man has in him this pre-existing dormant existence, which in the time of God's will is awakened, or quickened, or vivified, by the Holy Spirit acting on it, raising it into life, and that this process is the new birth.

The question is of great import in preaching to the heathen, for it is thus—if an entirely new creation occurs in the new birth, then a preacher stands before his congregation as a man before a garden with no seed in his hands, and he waits till God wills to give him seed to throw into the garden; while, if the new birth is the resurrection or quickening of a pre-existing dormant existence, the preacher stands before his congregation as a man before a garden full of seeds, which he has to water in order to vivify into life.

The preacher, in the latter case, is merely a conduit or channel of communication of the Holy Ghost to the dormant pre-existence; so also is the word of the scripture; the spirit is the quickener in both cases. If the preacher is worldly-minded, his channel of communication is clogged, and his preaching will be feeble.

It may be asked, How came this pre-existence to be dormant or dead? I consider that the soul of man existed first, and that it died, or became dormant, in Adam at the Fall; that, as all bodies were in the loins of Adam, so also were all souls in his soul, and that this soul, and all other souls, were breathed into Adam by God at his creation; in a word, they were all incarnated in him, to be developed in due time.

Death, or dormant state, fell on them all at the Fall; death is separation from God. Christ removed by His death the barrier of separation. The Veil being removed, God could shed forth His spirit on the dormant souls, and recall them to life, raise them from the dead, revivify them. It is difficult to say!—Are the souls of all men raised from their dormant state ere death falls on their bodies? I think they may be, even at the last moment; for what is the new birth or resurrection but the instantaneous awakening or rousing up of a dormant or dead existence?

It may be said that there are men who

lived such lives as would render it difficult to believe in their future salvation. To me this simply implies that the souls of such men are dormant, or so little quickened as to produce no influence on their outward conduct. I do not by this imply that the evil dispositions of men will inherit eternal life; but I mean that there is, in every man, what I call an essential existence, which, though dormant or dead for the time, is capable of, and is an inheritor of, eternal life. Man's judgment cannot be accepted in this matter; a renegade Christian native may plunge into great social wickedness—this shocks our social feelings, while the renegade European Christian may be guilty of all sorts of Satanic sins, and yet he will not be considered a social scandal; yet the one is guilty as an *animal*, the other as a *devil*.

I believe that the Divine Breathing into Adam (which Breathing made him differ from all animals) was the breathing into him of certain existences of God's nature; that these existences or souls were of God, as existing and derived from Him, and consequently God's; that in time each of these souls were incarnated in bodies, but that through the Fall these bodies with which they were clothed were sinful and had carnal desires; that the only difference between Christ and man is that, in the case of Christ, He was the fulness of the Godhead in a sinless body, and that man is of God (equally though inferiorly a son) in sinful flesh or body; that the Fall caused the death or dormant state to fall on all these souls, in which state they would have remained, unless Christ offered His body as a substitute for their bodies' transgressions.

In Adam all souls and bodies stood, fell, and died; in Christ all are made alive, or raised or awakened from a dormant state.

How then ought man to be exhorted? They need some hope to be before them; for even our Lord needed it when He, for the joy set before Him, endured the cross, despising the shame. I would point out to them the fact that they have God dwelling in them, a fact which only the man himself can know; and to the degree the preacher is devoid of self, so will this word be with power, and the hearer will realise the truth; the dormant Divine existence is awakened never to sleep again, and I believe that the now raised and quickened soul will grope its way out of its shell; it will contend with the body, often being nearly extinguished but never quite, till the body gives up the struggle in natural death.

The grand distinctive mark of the Christian religion, which causes it to differ from any other religion, is the indwelling of God in man. The expiation of Christ was the removal of a barrier which enabled man to regain his former union with God; the gift or renewal of the Holy Ghost was the result of His Passion. This was the " Promise of my Father, which," saith He, "ye have heard of Me." Union with God implies the very closest intimacy in heaven, and there can be no intimacy closer than the mutual indwelling of God in man and man in God.

The intricate curious formation of man's body prophesies some wonderful future to that raised body in a future state. Man could never be satisfied with less than God; his aspirations could not stop short of the infinite; and I believe that heaven and the future life is the exploration of the infinite mind of God; that our life on this earth is a drill-ground for a future active life, the seen things of which are connected with the unseen things of the next—the seeds of them.

If by the restraint of self, in some little apparent matter in the world, we avoid an immensely more severe struggle in the next, we should willingly restrain self here. This view makes everything seem important, whereas we generally think some things most important and others trivial.

What does God want from man? If thou sinnest, what doest thou against Him? If thou art righteous, what givest thou to Him? Thy wickedness may hurt thy fellow men, but it neither hurts nor benefits God thy Maker. It is as if God said, "In union with Me is thy happiness; in disunion is thy misery"; and man said, "I want Thy gifts, but not Thee; for I desire not the knowledge of Thy ways"; and that God replied, "My gifts without Me thou canst not have, for they are inseparable from Me." To wish for heaven, and not to desire union with God, is like wishing to live in a palace and to have nothing to say to its owners; and as heaven is God, this cannot be.

Men wish for the absence of evil from the earth, yet desire not the presence of God. They desire light without the Light of lights; they would take the things of darkness, together with light, when the presence of light destroys those things.

The fact that for seeds in nature to

sprout, both corruption and moisture are needed, suggests the deep thought that our spiritual growth, the growth of the soul, is derivable from the corruption of the body it is planted or incarnated in, when that soul is quickened by the Holy Ghost. Such an expression as " renewing of the Holy Ghost" implies a restoration of what has once been possessed and then lost; it does not imply a primary action. The fact is, that by the Fall man lost the Holy Ghost, by which he was in union with God, and by the redemption he regained the Holy Ghost, by which he is in renewed union with God.

Put a stone into manure, and water it, you will have no result; put a seed into earth, and water it, you will have a result. To my mind, the soul is a dormant seed, implanted or incarnated in corruption; on it rests the Holy Ghost, and the Holy Ghost develops the existing faculties, till then dormant, of the soul.

WARNING TO THE WATCHMEN.

Ezekiel iii. 17, 18.

"Ye are My watchmen; if thou dost not give thy flock warning, and they die in their sin, their blood will I require at thy hand."

These words to our first parents, "You "had the full warning of the effects of "disobeying My command, *not to eat*, con- "tinually, during your life before you:" should be changed for us into this saying of the Lord, I said to you, in words solemn enough to call your attention, "Verily, verily, except ye eat the flesh of the Son of Man, and drink His blood, ye have no life in you;" that I would raise him up who ate My flesh and blood at the last day; that I would dwell in him and he in Me; and I showed you how to eat My body and to drink My blood. Further, I asked you to do this in remembrance of Me; I told you, through My apostle Paul, that as oft as ye did this, ye showed forth My death for you. Therefore, you that will not obey My words, can have no wish for Me to

H

dwell in you. You disobey My command, you will not have Me in your remembrance, My death you care not to recognise, My table is contemptible, the meat, My body, is contemptible; "the table of the Lord is polluted: and the fruit thereof, even His meat, is contemptible" (Mal. i. 12). You prefer your purchases of ground, your oxen, your wives, to My table. Ye count the blood of the Covenant, My blood, a common thing. Not only hast thou broken My command, as you did in the beginning, but you have despised My death, which I underwent to deliver you from the effects of your first disobedience. I will say no more to you than that, as this is so, you shall not taste of My supper.

I gave you the charge of My Mysteries, I appointed you as overseers to My flock, I honoured you to administer these Mysteries to that flock. My words were clear as to what was to be done; equally clear was what I said would result from obeying My commands, and what would result from disobeying them. I said that any man, whosoever, that came to Me, I would receive. Your parents had My words, " In the day thou eatest thereof thou shalt die." Were not these words true? Did I explain how that eating would bring death? Have I ordered you to explain how My words to "take, eat," will enable Me to live in a man and he in Me? I told you that, if you ate in the beginning, you would die. Did I not speak truth? And now that I tell you that whoever eateth My body and drinketh My blood dwelleth in Me, do I speak a thing not to be credited, and require you to qualify My words with your explanations? My words to your father Adam were clear and distinct: " In the day thou eatest thou shalt die." My words to My flock, through you, My shepherds, are, " Take, eat; this is My body: do this in remembrance of Me." You say you fear that evil will come to your flock unless you explain; you hereby imply that I have given a command which needs your explanation to render obedience to it beneficial; that, unless you explain, My command may, by *being obeyed*, be an evil thing. I have anticipated this view by My words that *those who disobey My command* have *no life*. Do you reason that they who *obey My command* will be worse by doing so? I did not open out the misery of disobeying My first command, "Do not eat," but I have opened out the blessings of obedience of My second command, "Take, eat."

ON THE INDWELLING OF GOD IN US AS LIVING VESSELS.

Our Lord said, "Destroy this temple, and in three days I will raise it up," but "He spake of the temple of His body" in which He (the second Person of the Trinity) was incarnated. Think of this fully, then read 1 Cor. iii. 16, "Know ye not that ye are the temple of God, and that the spirit of God dwelleth in you?"

1 Cor. vi. 19, says, "Your body is the temple of the Holy Ghost." Now compare the two passages in St. John (ii. 19, 21) with those in Corinthians, and one cannot avoid the criticism that, as God the Son was incarnated, or dwelt in a temple of flesh, so the Holy Ghost dwells in a temple of flesh in believers—the Church or body of Christ. So that in reality God the Son, incarnated in holy flesh, redeems the unholy flesh in which the Holy Ghost is. The Passion in the flesh suffered by our Lord removed the curse from the flesh of man otherwise accursed, and, by the indwelling of the Holy Ghost in man, man believes unto salvation. The final result at the end of the world is, that God the Son is incarnated in the flesh (of which we do not doubt,) and that God the Holy Ghost is in the Church, which Church is the bride or body of Christ, and was redeemed by the Passion of Christ. There can be no question that the word "incarnation" (not a scriptural

one) is as applicable to the indwelling of the Holy Ghost in believers, as it is with respect to God the Son having taken flesh. Though the end of the world finds the Holy Ghost incarnate in the Church, and God the Son incarnate in the flesh, making one, no more twain—the new Adam and Eve—and though this state must continue for ever; yet the time when the Holy Ghost became incarnated in each believer is not so clear as the time when our Lord became incarnated at Nazareth. The relation between God the Son and His body must be the same as between God the Holy Ghost and the Church, or corporate body of believers. Our Lord was made flesh in time, and in a time known to us. He was not made flesh from all eternity. Therefore the Holy Ghost was incarnated in believers in time, and not from eternity.

Now, if I could, I would (humanly speaking) desire to leave the argument thus. But here is Hebrews ii. 14—

"Forasmuch as the children are partakers of flesh and blood" (viz. are incarnated) "He also Himself took part of the same" (became incarnated). By our Lord taking flesh He became man and able to suffer; by the children taking flesh they became man and able to suffer.

We find them at the end of the world reunited and in glorified flesh, as the Lamb's bride, the Church. We find at the end of the world the Lamb's bride, the Church, made up of many members, who are knit as one with one another, and with Christ, by the Holy Ghost who is their life, and whose withdrawal would be cessation of the life of the Church and of the union between Christ and His Church. In the one case the children are in the flesh, and, at the end of the world, make the Church of Christ. In the other case, the selfsame Church of Christ exists only by the incarnation or indwelling of the Holy Ghost. It seems difficult to avoid the conclusion that the "children" are, in some way from the first, of the "Holy Ghost." I can see no way to avoid this conclusion and its sequence, that God the Son was incarnated in holy flesh to redeem the unholy flesh, in which the children were incarnated after the fall.

I do not wish it to be understood that I think the souls of believers are of the Holy Ghost Alone (though they are the breath of God). I believe the souls of believers are of God. Our Lord was, and is, God the Son: He has a human soul and human body. This is scriptural. The only difficulty is, What is the soul? All we know of it is that it came from God's breathing, and that it animates the body, and is the personality of each believer. At the end of the world its state is known to us. It is in union with God the Holy Ghost, and by that union it is a member of Christ's body and a son of God. What it was before its incarnation is not so clear.

Comfort Bestowed through Reflection on our Pardon in Christ.

We are members of Christ's Body mystical, existent ere the worlds were made, yet fashioned in time. Our names are written in the Book of Life, yet may be blotted out (read Apocalypse iii. 5). These are things which even the angels desire to look into. We were incarnated in tabernacles over which Satan had power. We were incarnated in order to know God. These tabernacles, and our souls in them, have a leaning towards things of earth. Regard man for the moment as consisting of body and soul; though I accept the tripartite division which is given through Paul, of body, soul and spirit. Then we may say that in us the sins of the body are imputatively those of the soul—even as the sins of Christ's Body the Church are the sins of Christ, the Head of the Church. (Read Psalm lxix. 5, and many other passages.)

This is so by the cause of the decreed oneness of Body and Head.

As Christ, in virtue of His being God, is Saviour to His Church, so we in our souls, where the body and the spirit meet, are in virtue of our being Christ's members, saviours to our bodies. We daily present them in sacrifice (read Romans xii. 1, and read as carefully for our personality 1 Cor. vi. 20). The Divinity of Christ is a necessity to His being the Saviour— the membership of our souls with Christ is a necessity in our dealings with our bodies. Also observe that Christ's offering was His Body, and the sequence was the gift of the Holy Ghost, and the restoration of our union with Christ as God. I mention this as a key to what I write on these various matters, and assure you that these views have been held by me for years. To me the fact, that my soul is so united to my body that I know not which is my body, and which my soul, is a proof of the oneness of Christ with our souls, neither step being now visible as a definite step, while each is a step. This renders comprehensible Christ's complaint as to the sins he bore (Psalm lxix., &c.) ; not that I think for one moment He was ignorant as we are ignorant, with respect to the division between Him and us as God, while yet He is man. He did feel all the sorrow and grief as if He had really committed the offences for which He suffered. Judging from the exactitude of God in all things, I think that any idea that offences are forgotten, though forgiven, cannot be admitted, since our Lord suffered for every offence, and He would remember it from the suffering it caused. It is this transcendent love which would break our hearts in the end, were we not then to know that our offences were committed in ignorance, and were pardonable so far as they were in ignorance. This Saint Paul felt, and he knew, as we may know, that being enlightened we no longer take pleasure in them. We err in our hearts because we do not know His ways. We are not less blameworthy, for He has shewn us the way of life by His Scriptures.

I have a strong belief that our mental and other struggles here are the roots of larger forms of movement, or I might say of larger reflections of them, in other worlds : as for example, any word here may have momentous effects in other worlds; or any designed silence here, like Herod's at Cæsarea, may have as great an effect. I have also the strange belief that you, my friend, are in me and I in you in some manner not alien from these effects or reflections, consequently when we met, there was an increased life in us. Each learned from the other, each by the other learned more from Christ. I know this may be called fanciful, but it contains comfort. It cheers life to me. Now I find little to do except these studies, yet I know that in reality it is not so much the events of life in which we take our part, as it is intrinsically for each one the effort or manner in which we meet such events.

THE PASSION OF CHRIST THE HEAD OF THE CHURCH.

I remark in Eph. iii. 10 the statement that—" All things were created by Jesus Christ to the intent that *by the Church* the manifold wisdom of God should be made known to all powers and principalities in heavenly places." This passage always seemed to be so very strong, that *by the Church* (which is made up of such fearfully unclean, evil members,) God should choose to show forth His manifold wisdom, and to overturn evil. It, however, is a fresh light when one sees that the Church is the incarnation of the Holy Ghost. It manifests one thing, which is now past our comprehension, that the passion of our Lord must have been most stupendous, in order that such fearful sinners as men are should be so infinitely exalted.

Consider how very much we feel an unjust accusation, or, indeed, a just one. If any one says that X is a very selfish person, X will feel it bitterly, though X cannot deny it. X will try and make out he is not selfish. Imagine what our Lord went through with the imputations on Him in the midst of His terrible pain before the face of the whole universe. Try and realise the catalogue.

" Thou didst that, and that, and that." Add to it the taunts of the Jews.

" Save Thyself, and come down from the cross."

Add the exquisite sensitiveness of our Lord to anything like sin. The feeling that He was guilty, for it was His body (the Church) who committed these offences. The intense temptation to justify Himself and give us up, and cause the crash of the universe in one instant. He had the power to do it had He willed. The horror with which the angels looked on the personification of all our vileness; for He was made a curse for us. Truly it was stupendous.

I now use much the prayer—

"That He should recall to mind His trials, in order that, having paid the ransom for us, His enemies should not rise from their overthrow, and triumph over Him in us, His members."

I have before said that the sufferings, mental and physical, of our Lord, as *Head*, equal the sufferings, mental and physical, of the Church (past, present, and future), which is *His Body*. This Paul alludes to in Col. i. 24.

Christ, *our Head*, has gone through His suffering; but Christ, in His body, the Church, is still suffering. I am Jesus, whose *body* thou art persecuting. It is *Me*. Why persecutest thou *Me*, my body, the Church? The more you are persecuted by your enemies, by your flesh, the more share you take of the sum total of the Church's suffering, His body, and the more vital are you as a member of that body.

To be free from suffering in the flesh would be impossible for any member of Christ's body. Such suffering from our enemies in the flesh is a certain sign of membership, when such suffering is undergone by those who wish for holiness and have it not in the measure they desire.

It is difficult to see how a believer becomes a member of Christ, of His body, the Church. Scripture shows us that this membership depends on and is caused by the indwelling or, if we dare use this word, *incarnation* of the Holy Ghost; but what purifying power must there be from that indwelling to render any believer *spotless* before God, having His own righteousness! Everything we possess must be got rid of ere that sanctity is reached! and we can scarcely expect that anything or any part of us can exist under such circumstances. If we had new bodies altogether it would be easier to understand, but Paul speaks of being *clothed upon*, not *unclothed*, and the Heavenly body is certainly the issue or outcome of the earthly body. My mind turns on whether in us, believers, the term *Me* is not the Holy Ghost Himself. Then I can understand all, for then the Nephesh, his "animal" soul (and the bodies it is one with), having been redeemed by Christ, can be knit to the term *Me*, the Holy Ghost in us, and be perfectly holy, viz. a new creature through resurrection from the dead. I cannot help thinking that it is so, viz. that when we are believers, and consequently members of Christ, our term *Me* is one, with the Holy Ghost in us, and the life we live, the life of the Holy Ghost. I know this is not clear; but if we look at the Scriptures we see that the shredding-off process is conspicuous, also the continual renewal. It was one continual pruning with the Israelites; a remnant alone remains. Paul speaks of the attaining to the resurrection of the dead.

I imagine he alludes to attaining the power of the resurrection life ere his actual death. Here is the question. We were sinners and dead. A barrier existed between God the Father and us; Christ came and redeemed us and removed the barrier, and God the Holy Ghost comes and dwells in us (note that word dwell, for it is the same as incarnate), and gives us life and union with Christ. He prunes us down and sanctifies us for that union. He hews and cuts the stones of His temple, casting out the evil in us. He carries out the work with infinite power. We are one with Him and have His righteousness, which is God's, both Father, Son, and Holy Ghost. We owe all this especially to Christ Jesus, the God and Man, who suffered for us; therefore, though we owe great gratitude to God the Father and God the Holy Ghost, we owe still more to Christ Jesus, for He actually suffered for us in His flesh. Christ, as God, did *not* suffer; the Holy Ghost, a

God, does not suffer; we, as men, suffer to a certain degree. Christ's sufferings are expiatory; our sufferings are sequences of our sins, and for our discipline. Christ's sufferings are the full, perfect, and sufficient sacrifice, oblation, and satisfaction for the sins of the world, made once and for ever on the cross. Our sufferings are disciplinary, not expiatory; yet I believe the sum of these disciplinary sufferings (suffered from the beginning to the end of the world by the Church, His body) equal the sum of those expiatory sufferings undergone by Christ, the Head of the Church, on the cross. Our Lord bore the imputation and punishment of every sin in those three hours of terrible physical suffering. Satan and his host applied to Him the taunt of every sin ever committed, and this in the face of all the universe. Now realise our feelings when we are unjustly accused by perhaps one person, when we know we are not perfect, and then imagine what He went through on the cross, Naked, and apparently to us even by God the Father, Deserted, with the accusations of all those offences cast at Him. Truly it was fearful ! Fancy if we had our catalogue investigated, even by the nearest of our kin; could we even then imagine what He went through ? He was satisfied with the travail of His soul, so if the sacrifice He went through was, to His mind, commensurate with the result of such suffering, how great must be that result of His Passion ! One great thing in prayer is, " O my God, remember the sufferings of Thy Son, Thy darling (Yachidah), and suffer not the world, flesh, or devil to render those sufferings nugatory, or useless by letting those enemies triumph over the members of His body, which by Thy Holy Ghost dwelling in us Thou hast made us to be." Rejoice not for anything but one —that your name is written in heaven !

Our Lord's words were, Father, into Thy

hands I commit or put in trust My spirit. He slept, and from His side came forth the Church, by its symbols the water and blood.

It is remarkable that the Jews, always on going to bed made this prayer—

Blessed be God in the day, blessed be God in the night. Blessed be God in our lying down, blessed be God in our rising up; in Thy hands are the breath of all living and the souls of all who die; in Thy hands are the souls [nephesh] of every living being and the spirit [ruach] of every man. Into Thy hand do I commit my spirit [ruach]. Oh! Thou true upright God, redeem me. Oh! God and Heavenly Father, Thy name and kingdom endureth for ever, Thou shalt reign over us for ever. *Amen.*

When they got up, they prayed thus—

I acknowledge with thanks before Thee, O King, that liveth and existeth together, that Thou, in mercy, hath caused my breath [neshamah] to return to me. Thy truth is very great; the fear of the

Lord is the beginning of wisdom, and good understanding to all who do Thy will; Thy praise endureth for ever. Blessed be His name for ever and ever. *Amen.*

All the young Jews, from time immemorial, used these prayers, and the Jews near the Cross knew what our Lord meant when He said, "Into thy hand I commit my spirit." He was going to sleep.

The Jews, in their prayer, gave over their spirits to God to take care of, as little children confide their treasures to their mother at night.

The following has comforted me. Do not abhor us, for Thy Name's sake. Do not disgrace the Throne of Thy glory: Remember, Break not Thy Covenant with us (Jeremiah xiv. 21). My comfort in this passage is based (1) on the words that if we believe in Jesus, He dwells in us, and we are His members—members of His Body; and based (2) on the fact that if a promise is made me by one

" who knows, even to the anatomy of the backbone " [this is an expression used by Bishop Wordsworth to denote God's knowledge of us], then I have a right not only to believe that promise, but I am dishonouring the Promiser if I do not. We have the right, indeed it is our duty, to pray with this claim. I pray thus: " Art Thou forgetful of what Thine enemies have made Thee to suffer of Thy victory over them that Thou allowest the members of Thy Body to fall under the power of Thine enemies, and then to triumph over Thee in Thy members? Will not Thine enemies exult if they conquer Thy members? Wilt Thou disgrace the Throne of Thy glory? Wilt Thou forget Thy covenant with us into which Thou hast entered, for Thou, O Lord, knowest all concerning Thy members?" This is my prayer— the prayer that the simplest of us can make.

You believe in your heart that Jesus is

the Son of God? Then God dwells in your body, and if you ask Him, "O Lord! I believe that Jesus is the Son of God; shew me, for His sake, that Thou livest in me," He will make you feel His presence in your heart. Many believe sincerely that Jesus is the Son of God, but are not happy, because they do not believe that which God tells them: that He lives in them, both in body and soul, if they confess Jesus to be His Son. You believe this statement, yet do not feel God's presence? Ask Him to shew Himself to you and He will surely do so.

O Lord, who dost live in all who believe that Jesus is Thy Son, make us feel Thy presence more and more, and grant that the Holy Ghost may produce, by His indwelling in us, more of the fruit of our union with our Lord and Saviour, to Thy honour and glory. *Amen.*

Characters in Holy Scripture.

We should read the Bible lovingly, and thereby make a fair and just allowance (which does us good), for many of the characters are therein described faithfully for our good. I am thinking of Abraham, of the people of Ziph, of David, and others.

ABRAHAM. — Treachery is our great fault, so consequently the world is celebrated for that vice, and the true Zion is celebrated for sincerity. The words of God to Abraham were: "I am Thy shield, and Thy exceeding great reward. .... Be thou perfect, that is, sincere" [Thamim, Genesis xvii. 1]. Abraham does not hesitate, he comes out at once with what is in his mind. He will trust the promise at once. He virtually says, "This is very well, but Sarah and I am old." It is all full of the wealth of that verse which pervades both the Old Testament and the New: "He believed in the Lord, and He counted it to him for righteousness." How delightful all this is! and how simple! This is the way to teach our lambs to pray. How empty are the mass of our prayers! How often are we found praying for the Holy Spirit, when we have Him in us, but do not care to acknowledge His Presence! We fence and guard the Gospel until it is no Gospel. Every one of those lambs in our Sunday schools we have the right to think of as God's lambs, for they are baptised into His Name. They are always in the presence of the Father, and we must help them to love Him and to be sincere. Treachery is the fault we are resisting. Their prayers offered sincerely move the lever of the world. They possess the eternal treasures, and they are able by their little prayers to confer greater benefits than any kings can; yet we in our folly often think we must so fence the Gospel as to paint for them the horrors of hell. Yet this we surely need not, ought not to do, because these horrors they know already, since the sense of evil is in us.

ZIPH.—I am highly delighted with the presumptive evidence fixing the place of Saul's anointing, and the place of Samuel's sacrifice. To me the land of Ziph and the Ziphites are lifelike. You have an orchard; just now the apples are getting ripe. You see a boy—any boy—hanging about that orchard. It needs no revelation to know what that boy is after; neither is it at all surprising that the gardener's boy should be likely to feel that he may get accused of aiding and abetting, and consequently may come and say, "So-and-So is always hanging about." The Ziphites were afraid of being compromised. They lived on their land. David was off at a moment's notice, and free of care. Not so with them—they could not move like that; consequently, they denounced David, but ought not to be hardly judged, as they often are. Treachery—the worst treachery—is of a deeper sort than was theirs.

DAVID.—David's character is one of no deceit, except about (1) the Philistines, and (2) Uriah; but even in those cases—I say, even in his deceit—he relied on God. David had an imperfect knowledge. David did not like the Philistines. In this he was right; and he wanted to destroy them. If we knew well the outline of Bible history, we could soon fill it out by the help of the Spirit of Love.

THE END.

www.ingramcontent.com/pod-product-compliance
Lightning Source LLC
Chambersburg PA
CBHW030400170426
43202CB00010B/1438